THE AU[TOBIOGRAPHY]
OF CHARLES DARWIN

FROM THE LIFE AND LETTERS OF CHARLES DARWIN

by

CHARLES DARWIN

COMPASS CIRCLE

The Autobiography Of Charles Darwin.
Current edition published by Compass Circle in 2019.

Published by Compass Circle
A Division of Garcia & Kitzinger Pty Ltd
Cover copyright ©2019 by Compass Circle.

Note:
All efforts have been made to preserve original spellings and punctuation of the original edition which may include old-fashioned English spellings of words and archaic variants.

This book is a product of its time and does not reflect the same views on race, gender, sexuality, ethnicity, and interpersonal relations as it would if it were written today.

For information contact :
information@compass-circle.com

It is not the strongest of the species that survives,
not the most intelligent that survives.
It is the one that is the most adaptable to change.

CHARLES DARWIN

SECRET WISDOM OF THE AGES SERIES

Life presents itself, it advances in a fast way. Life indeed never stops. It never stops until the end. The most diverse questions peek and fade in our minds. Sometimes we seek for answers. Sometimes we just let time go by.

The book you have now in your hands has been waiting to be discovered by you. This book may reveal the answers to some of your questions.

Books are friends. Friends who are always by your side and who can give you great ideas, advice or just comfort your soul. A great book can make you see things in your soul that you have not yet discovered, make you see things in your soul that you were not aware of.

Great books can change your life for the better. They can make you understand fascinating theories, give you new ideas, inspire you to undertake new challenges or to walk along new paths.

Life philosophies like the one of Charles Darwin, Henry Ford, John D. Rockefeller, Benjamin Franklin, Adam Smith, among others, are indeed a secret to many, but for those of us lucky enough to have discovered them, by one way or another, these books can enlighten us. They can open a wide range of possibilities to us. Because achieving greatness requires knowledge.

The series SECRET WISDOM OF THE AGES presented by Compass Circle try to bring you the great timeless masterpieces of personal development, positive thinking, and the law of attraction.

We welcome you to discover with us fascinating works by Henry Ford, John D. Rockefeller, Benjamin Franklin, Adam Smith, Wallace Wattles, Thomas Troward, James Allen, among others.

Contents

Editor's Note

My father's autobiographical recollections, given in the present chapter, were written for his children, —and written without any thought that they would ever be published. To many this may seem an impossibility; but those who knew my father will understand how it was not only possible, but natural. The autobiography bears the heading, 'Recollections of the Development of my Mind and Character,' and end with the following note:— "Aug. 3, 1876. This sketch of my life was begun about May 28th at Hopedene (Mr. Hensleigh Wedgwood's house in Surrey.), and since then I have written for nearly an hour on most afternoons." It will easily be understood that, in a narrative of a personal and intimate kind written for his wife and children, passages should occur which must here be omitted; and I have not thought it necessary to indicate where such omissions are made. It has been found necessary to make a few corrections of obvious verbal slips, but the number of such alterations has been kept down to the minimum.

—F.D.[*]

---

[*]Francis Darwin

Recollections Of The Development Of My Mind And Character

A German Editor having written to me for an account of the development of my mind and character with some sketch of my autobiography, I have thought that the attempt would amuse me, and might possibly interest my children or their children. I know that it would have interested me greatly to have read even so short and dull a sketch of the mind of my grandfather, written by himself, and what he thought and did, and how he worked. I have attempted to write the following account of myself, as if I were a dead man in another world looking back at my own life. Nor have I found this difficult, for life is nearly over with me. I have taken no pains about my style of writing.

I was born at Shrewsbury on February 12th, 1809, and my earliest recollection goes back only to when I was a few months over four years old, when we went to near Abergele for sea-bathing, and I recollect some events and places there with some little distinctness.

My mother died in July 1817, when I was a little over eight years old, and it is odd that I can remember hardly anything about her except her death-bed, her black velvet gown, and her curiously constructed work-table. In the spring of this same year I was sent to a day-school in Shrewsbury, where I stayed a year. I have been told that I was much slower in learning than my younger sister Catherine, and I believe that I was in many ways a naughty boy.

By the time I went to this day-school (Kept by Rev. G. Case, minister of the Unitarian Chapel in the High Street. Mrs. Darwin was a Unitarian and attended Mr. Case's chapel, and my father as a little boy went there with his elder sisters. But both he and his brother were christened and intended to belong to the Church of England; and after his early boyhood he seems usually to have gone to church and not to Mr. Case's. It appears ("St. James' Gazette", Dec. 15, 1883) that a mural tablet has been erected to his memory in the chapel, which is now known as the 'Free Christian Church.') my taste for natural history, and more especially for collecting, was well developed. I tried to make out the names of plants (Rev. W.A. Leighton, who was a schoolfellow of my father's at Mr. Case's school, remembers his bringing a flower to school and saying that his mother had taught him how by looking at the inside of the blossom the name of the plant could be discovered. Mr. Leighton goes on, "This greatly roused my attention and curiosity, and I enquired of him repeatedly how this could be done?"—but his lesson was naturally enough not transmissible.—F.D.), and collected all sorts of things, shells, seals, franks, coins, and minerals. The passion for collecting which leads a man to be a systematic naturalist, a virtuoso, or a miser, was very strong in me, and was clearly innate, as none of my sisters or brother ever had this taste.

One little event during this year has fixed itself very firmly in my mind, and I hope that it has done so from my conscience having been afterwards sorely troubled by it; it is curious as showing that apparently I was interested at this early age in the variability of plants! I told another little boy (I believe it was Leighton, who afterwards became a well-known lichenologist and botanist), that I could produce variously coloured polyanthuses and primroses by watering them with certain coloured fluids, which was of course a monstrous fable, and had never been tried by me. I may here also confess that as a little boy I was much given to inventing deliberate falsehoods, and this was always done for the sake of causing excitement. For instance, I once gathered much valuable fruit from my father's trees and hid it in the shrubbery, and then ran in breathless haste to spread the news that I had discovered a hoard of stolen fruit.

I must have been a very simple little fellow when I first went to the school. A boy of the name of Garnett took me into a cake shop one day, and bought some cakes for which he did not pay, as the shopman trusted him. When we came out I asked him why he did not pay for them, and he instantly answered, "Why, do you not know that my uncle left a great sum of money to the town on condition that every tradesman should give whatever was wanted without payment to any one who wore his old hat and moved [it] in a particular manner?" and he then showed me how it was moved. He then went into another shop where he was trusted, and asked for some small article, moving his hat in the proper manner, and of course obtained it without payment. When we came out he said, "Now if you like to go by yourself into that cake-shop (how well I remember its exact position) I will lend you my hat, and you can get whatever you like if you move the hat on your head properly." I gladly accepted the generous offer, and went in and asked for some cakes, moved the old hat and was walking out of the shop, when the shopman made a rush at me, so I dropped the cakes and ran for dear life, and was astonished by being greeted with shouts of laughter by my false friend Garnett.

I can say in my own favour that I was as a boy humane, but I owed this entirely to the instruction and example of my sisters. I doubt indeed whether humanity is a natural or innate quality. I was very fond of collecting eggs, but I never took more than a single egg out of a bird's nest, except on one single occasion, when I took all, not for their value, but from a sort of bravado.

I had a strong taste for angling, and would sit for any number of hours on the bank of a river or pond watching the float; when at Maer (The house of his uncle, Josiah Wedgwood.) I was told that I could kill the worms with salt and water, and from that day I never spitted a living worm, though at the expense probably of some loss of success.

Once as a very little boy whilst at the day school, or before that time, I acted cruelly, for I beat a puppy, I believe, simply from enjoying the sense of power; but the beating could not have been severe, for the puppy did not howl, of which I feel sure, as the spot was near the house. This act lay heavily on my conscience, as is shown by my remembering the exact spot where the crime was committed. It probably lay all the heavier from my love of dogs being then, and for a long time afterwards, a passion. Dogs seemed to know this, for I was an adept in robbing their love from their masters.

I remember clearly only one other incident during this year whilst at Mr. Case's daily school,— namely, the burial of a dragoon soldier; and it is surprising how clearly I can still see the horse with the man's empty boots and carbine suspended to the saddle, and the firing over the grave. This scene deeply stirred whatever poetic fancy there was in me.

In the summer of 1818 I went to Dr. Butler's great school in Shrewsbury, and remained there for seven years still Midsummer 1825, when I was sixteen years old. I boarded at this school, so that I had the great advantage of living the life of a true schoolboy; but as the distance was hardly more than a mile to my home, I very often ran there in the longer intervals between the callings over and before locking up at night. This, I think, was in many ways advantageous to me by keeping up home affections and interests. I remember in the early part of my school life that I often had to run very quickly to be in time, and from being a fleet runner was generally successful; but when in doubt I prayed earnestly to God to help me, and I well remember that I attributed my success to the prayers and not to my quick running, and marvelled how generally I was aided.

I have heard my father and elder sister say that I had, as a very young boy, a strong taste for long solitary walks; but what I thought about I know not. I often became quite absorbed, and once, whilst returning to school on the summit of the old fortifications round Shrewsbury, which had been converted into a public foot-path with no parapet on one side, I walked off and fell to the ground, but the height was only seven or eight feet. Nevertheless the number of thoughts which passed through my mind during this very short, but sudden and wholly unexpected fall, was astonishing, and seem hardly compatible with what physiologists have, I believe, proved about each thought requiring quite an appreciable amount of time.

Nothing could have been worse for the development of my mind than Dr. Butler's school, as it was strictly classical, nothing else being taught, except a little ancient geography and history. The school as a means of education to me was simply a blank. During my whole life I have been singularly incapable of mastering any language. Especial attention was paid to verse-making, and this I could never do well. I had many friends, and got together a good collection of old verses, which by patching together, sometimes aided by other boys, I could work into any subject. Much attention was paid to learning by heart the lessons of the previous day; this I could effect with great facility, learning forty or fifty lines of Virgil or Homer, whilst I was in morning chapel; but this exercise was utterly useless, for every verse was forgotten in forty-eight hours. I was not idle, and with the exception of versification, generally worked conscientiously at my classics, not using cribs. The sole pleasure I ever received from such studies, was from some of the odes of Horace, which I admired greatly.

When I left the school I was for my age neither high nor low in it; and I believe that I was considered by all my masters and by my father as a very ordinary boy, rather below the common standard in intellect. To my deep mortification my father once said to me, "You care for nothing but shooting, dogs, and rat-catching, and you will be a disgrace to yourself and all your family." But my father, who was the kindest man I ever knew and whose memory I love with all my heart, must have been angry and somewhat unjust when he used such words.

Looking back as well as I can at my character during my school life, the only qualities which at this period promised well for the future, were, that I had strong and diversified tastes, much zeal for whatever interested me, and a keen pleasure in understanding any complex subject or thing. I was taught Euclid by a private tutor, and I distinctly remember the intense satisfaction which the clear geometrical proofs gave me. I remember, with equal distinctness, the delight which my uncle gave me (the father of Francis Galton) by explaining the principle of the vernier of a barometer with respect to diversified tastes, independently of science, I was fond of reading various books, and I used to sit for hours reading the historical plays of Shakespeare, generally in an old window in the thick walls of the school. I read also other poetry, such as Thomson's 'Seasons,' and the recently published poems of Byron and Scott. I mention this because later in life I wholly lost, to my great regret, all pleasure from poetry of any kind, including Shakespeare. In connection with pleasure from poetry, I may add that in 1822 a vivid delight in scenery was first awakened in my mind, during a riding tour on the borders of Wales, and this has lasted longer than any other aesthetic pleasure.

Early in my school days a boy had a copy of the 'Wonders of the World,' which I often read, and disputed with other boys about the veracity of some of the statements; and I believe that this book first gave me a wish to travel in remote countries, which was ultimately fulfilled by the voyage of the "Beagle". In the latter part of my school life I became passionately fond of shooting; I do not believe that any one could have shown more zeal for the most holy cause than I did for shooting birds. How well I remember killing my first snipe, and my excitement was so great that I had much difficulty in reloading my gun from the trembling of my hands. This taste long continued, and I became a very good shot. When at Cambridge I used to practise throwing up my gun to my shoulder before a looking-glass to see that I threw it up straight. Another and better plan was to get a friend to wave about a lighted candle, and then to fire at it with a cap on the nipple, and if the aim was accurate the little puff of air would blow out the candle. The explosion of the cap caused a sharp crack, and I was told that the tutor of the college remarked, "What an extraordinary thing it is, Mr. Darwin seems to spend hours in cracking a horse-whip in his room, for I often hear the crack when I pass under his windows."

I had many friends amongst the schoolboys, whom I loved dearly, and I think that my disposition was then very affectionate.

With respect to science, I continued collecting minerals with much zeal, but quite unscientifically— all that I cared about was a new-*named* mineral, and I hardly attempted to classify them. I must have observed insects with some little care, for when ten years old (1819) I went for three weeks to Plas Edwards on the sea-coast in Wales, I was very much interested and surprised at seeing a large black and scarlet Hemipterous insect, many moths (Zygaena), and a Cicindela which are not found in Shropshire. I almost made up my mind to begin collecting all the insects which I could find dead, for on consulting my sister I concluded that it was not right to kill insects for the sake of making a collection. From reading White's 'Selborne,' I took much pleasure in watching the habits of birds, and even made notes on the subject. In my simplicity I remember wondering why every gentleman did not become an ornithologist.

Towards the close of my school life, my brother worked hard at chemistry, and made a fair laboratory with proper apparatus in the tool-house in the garden, and I was allowed to aid him as a servant in most of his experiments. He made all the gases and many compounds, and I read with great care several books on chemistry, such as Henry and Parkes' 'Chemical Catechism.' The subject interested me greatly, and we often used to go on working till rather late at night. This was the best part of my education at school, for it showed me practically the meaning of experimental science. The fact that we worked at chemistry somehow got known at school, and as it was an unprecedented fact, I was nicknamed "Gas." I was also once publicly rebuked by the head-master, Dr. Butler, for thus wasting my time on such useless subjects; and he called me very unjustly a "poco curante," and as I did not understand what he meant, it seemed to me a fearful reproach.

As I was doing no good at school, my father wisely took me away at a rather earlier age than usual, and sent me (Oct. 1825) to Edinburgh University with my brother, where I stayed for two years or sessions. My brother was completing his medical studies, though I do not believe he ever really intended to practise, and I was sent there to commence them. But soon after this period I became convinced from various small circumstances that my father would leave me property enough to subsist on with some comfort, though I never imagined that I should be so rich a man as I am; but my belief was sufficient to check any strenuous efforts to learn medicine.

The instruction at Edinburgh was altogether by lectures, and these were intolerably dull, with the exception of those on chemistry by Hope; but to my mind there are no advantages and many disadvantages in lectures compared with reading. Dr. Duncan's lectures on Materia Medica at 8 o'clock on a winter's morning are something fearful to remember. Dr.—— made his lectures on human anatomy as dull as he was himself, and the subject disgusted me. It has proved one of the greatest evils in my life that I was not urged to practise dissection, for I should soon have got over my disgust; and the practice would have been invaluable for all my future work. This has been an irremediable evil, as well as my incapacity to draw. I also attended regularly the clinical wards in the hospital. Some of the cases distressed me a good deal, and I still have vivid pictures before me of some of them; but I was not so foolish as to allow this to lessen my attendance. I cannot understand why this part of my medical course did not interest me in a greater degree; for during the summer before coming to Edinburgh I began attending some of the poor people, chiefly children and women in Shrewsbury: I wrote down as full an account as I could of the case with all the symptoms, and read them aloud to my father, who suggested further inquiries and advised me what medicines to give, which I made up myself. At one time I had at least a dozen patients, and I felt a keen interest in the work. My father, who was by far the best judge of character whom I ever knew, declared that I should make a successful physician,—meaning by this one who would get many patients. He maintained that the chief element of success was exciting confidence; but what he saw in me which convinced him that I should create confidence I know not. I also attended on two occasions the operating theatre in the hospital at Edinburgh, and saw two very bad operations, one on a child, but I rushed away before they were completed. Nor did I ever attend again, for hardly any inducement would have been strong enough to make me do so; this being long before the blessed days of chloroform. The two cases fairly haunted me for many a long year.

My brother stayed only one year at the University, so that during the second year I was left to my own resources; and this was an advantage, for I became well acquainted with several young men fond of natural science. One of these was Ainsworth, who afterwards published his travels in Assyria; he was a Wernerian geologist, and knew a little about many subjects. Dr. Coldstream was a very different young man, prim, formal, highly religious, and most kind-hearted; he afterwards published some good zoological articles. A third young man was Hardie, who would, I think, have made a good botanist, but died early in India. Lastly, Dr. Grant, my senior by several years, but how I became acquainted with him I cannot remember; he published some first-rate zoological papers, but after coming to London as Professor in University College, he did nothing more in science, a fact which has always been inexplicable to me. I knew him well; he was dry and formal in manner, with much enthusiasm beneath this outer crust. He one day, when we were walking together, burst forth in high admiration of Lamarck and his views on evolution. I listened in silent astonishment, and as far as I can judge without any effect on my mind. I had previously read the 'Zoonomia' of my grandfather, in which similar views are maintained, but without producing any effect on me. Nevertheless it is probable that the hearing rather early in life such views maintained and praised may have favoured my upholding them under a different form in my 'Origin of Species.' At this time I admired greatly the 'Zoonomia;' but on reading it a second time after an interval of ten or fifteen years, I was much disappointed; the proportion of speculation being so large to the facts given.

Drs. Grant and Coldstream attended much to marine Zoology, and I often accompanied the former to collect animals in the tidal pools, which I dissected as well as I could. I also became friends with some of the Newhaven fishermen, and sometimes accompanied them when they trawled for oysters, and thus got many specimens. But from not having had any regular practice in dissection, and from possessing only a wretched microscope, my attempts were very poor. Nevertheless I made one interesting little discovery, and read, about the beginning of the year 1826, a short paper on the subject before the Plinian Society. This was that the so-called ova of Flustra had the power of independent movement by means of cilia, and were in fact larvae. In another short paper I showed that the little globular bodies which had been supposed to be the young state of Fucus loreus were the egg-cases of the wormlike Pontobdella muricata.

The Plinian Society was encouraged and, I believe, founded by Professor Jameson: it consisted of students and met in an underground room in the University for the sake of reading papers on natural science and discussing them. I used regularly to attend, and the meetings had a good effect on me in stimulating my zeal and giving me new congenial acquaintances. One evening a poor young man got up, and after stammering for a prodigious length of time, blushing crimson, he at last slowly got out the words, "Mr. President, I have forgotten what I was going to say." The poor fellow looked quite overwhelmed, and all the members were so surprised that no one could think of a word to say to cover his confusion. The papers which were read to our little society were not printed, so that I had not the satisfaction of seeing my paper in print; but I believe Dr. Grant noticed my small discovery in his excellent memoir on Flustra.

I was also a member of the Royal Medical Society, and attended pretty regularly; but as the subjects were exclusively medical, I did not much care about them. Much rubbish was talked there, but there were some good speakers, of whom the best was the present Sir J. Kay-Shuttleworth. Dr. Grant took me occasionally to the meetings of the Wernerian Society, where various papers on natural history were read, discussed, and afterwards published in the 'Transactions.' I heard Audubon deliver there some interesting discourses on the habits of N. American birds, sneering somewhat unjustly at Waterton. By the way, a negro lived in Edinburgh, who had travelled with Waterton, and gained his livelihood by stuffing birds, which he did excellently: he gave me lessons for payment, and I used often to sit with him, for he was a very pleasant and intelligent man.

Mr. Leonard Horner also took me once to a meeting of the Royal Society of Edinburgh, where I saw Sir Walter Scott in the chair as President, and he apologised to the meeting as not feeling fitted for such a position. I looked at him and at the whole scene with some awe and reverence, and I think it was owing to this visit during my youth, and to my having attended the Royal Medical Society, that I felt the honour of being elected a few years ago an honorary member of both these Societies, more than any other similar honour. If I had been told at that time that I should one day have been thus honoured, I declare that I should have thought it as ridiculous and improbable, as if I had been told that I should be elected King of England.

During my second year at Edinburgh I attended ——'s lectures on Geology and Zoology, but they were incredibly dull. The sole effect they produced on me was the determination never as long as I lived to read a book on Geology, or in any way to study the science. Yet I feel sure that I was prepared for a philosophical treatment of the subject; for an old Mr. Cotton in Shropshire, who knew a good deal about rocks, had pointed out to me two or three years previously a well-known large erratic boulder in the town of Shrewsbury, called the "bell-stone"; he told me that there was no rock of the same kind nearer than Cumberland or Scotland, and he solemnly assured me that the world would come to an end before any one would be able to explain how this stone came where it now lay. This produced a deep impression on me, and I meditated over this wonderful stone. So that I felt the keenest delight when I first read of the action of icebergs in transporting boulders, and I gloried in the progress of Geology. Equally striking is the fact that I, though now only sixty-seven years old, heard the Professor, in a field lecture at Salisbury Craigs, discoursing on a trapdyke, with amygdaloidal margins and the strata indurated on each side, with volcanic rocks all around us, say that it was a fissure filled with sediment from above, adding with a sneer that there were men who maintained that it had been injected from beneath in a molten condition. When I think of this lecture, I do not wonder that I determined never to attend to Geology.

From attending ——'s lectures, I became acquainted with the curator of the museum, Mr. Macgillivray, who afterwards published a large and excellent book on the birds of Scotland. I had much interesting natural-history talk with him, and he was very kind to me. He gave me some rare shells, for I at that time collected marine mollusca, but with no great zeal.

My summer vacations during these two years were wholly given up to amusements, though I always had some book in hand, which I read with interest. During the summer of 1826 I took a long walking tour with two friends with knapsacks on our backs through North wales. We walked thirty miles most days, including one day the ascent of Snowdon. I also went with my sister a riding tour in North Wales, a servant with saddle-bags carrying our clothes. The autumns were devoted to shooting chiefly at Mr. Owen's, at Woodhouse, and at my Uncle Jos's (Josiah Wedgwood, the son of the founder of the Etruria Works.) at Maer. My zeal was so great that I used to place my shooting-boots open by my bed-side when I went to bed, so as not to lose half a minute in putting them on in the morning; and on one occasion I reached a distant part of the Maer estate, on the 20th of August for black-game shooting, before I could see: I then toiled on with the game-keeper the whole day through thick heath and young Scotch firs.

I kept an exact record of every bird which I shot throughout the whole season. One day when shooting at Woodhouse with Captain Owen, the eldest son, and Major Hill, his cousin, afterwards Lord Berwick, both of whom I liked very much, I thought myself shamefully used, for every time after I had fired and thought that I had killed a bird, one of the two acted as if loading his gun, and cried out, "You must not count that bird, for I fired at the same time," and the gamekeeper, perceiving the joke, backed them up. After some hours they told me the joke, but it was no joke to me, for I had shot a large number of birds, but did not know how many, and could not add them to my list, which I used to do by making a knot in a piece of string tied to a button-hole. This my wicked friends had perceived.

How I did enjoy shooting! But I think that I must have been half-consciously ashamed of my zeal, for I tried to persuade myself that shooting was almost an intellectual employment; it required so much skill to judge where to find most game and to hunt the dogs well.

One of my autumnal visits to Maer in 1827 was memorable from meeting there Sir J. Mackintosh, who was the best converser I ever listened to. I heard afterwards with a glow of pride that he had said, "There is something in that young man that interests me." This must have been chiefly due to his perceiving that I listened with much interest to everything which he said, for I was as ignorant as a pig about his subjects of history, politics, and moral philosophy. To hear of praise from an eminent person, though no doubt apt or certain to excite vanity, is, I think, good for a young man, as it helps to keep him in the right course.

My visits to Maer during these two or three succeeding years were quite delightful, independently of the autumnal shooting. Life there was perfectly free; the country was very pleasant for walking or riding; and in the evening there was much very agreeable conversation, not so personal as it generally is in large family parties, together with music. In the summer the whole family used often to sit on the steps of the old portico, with the flower-garden in front, and with the steep wooded bank opposite the house reflected in the lake, with here and there a fish rising or a water-bird paddling about. Nothing has left a more vivid picture on my mind than these evenings at Maer. I was also attached to and greatly revered my Uncle Jos; he was silent and reserved, so as to be a rather awful man; but he sometimes talked openly with me. He was the very type of an upright man, with the clearest judgment. I do not believe that any power on earth could have made him swerve an inch from what he considered the right course. I used to apply to him in my mind the well-known ode of Horace, now forgotten by me, in which the words "nec vultus tyranni, etc.,"* come in.

---

*Justum et tenacem propositi virum
Non civium ardor prava jubentium
Non vultus instantis tyranni
Mente quatit solida.

Cambridge 1828-1831

After having spent two sessions in Edinburgh, my father perceived, or he heard from my sisters, that I did not like the thought of being a physician, so he proposed that I should become a clergyman. He was very properly vehement against my turning into an idle sporting man, which then seemed my probable destination. I asked for some time to consider, as from what little I had heard or thought on the subject I had scruples about declaring my belief in all the dogmas of the Church of England; though otherwise I liked the thought of being a country clergyman. Accordingly I read with care 'Pearson on the Creed,' and a few other books on divinity; and as I did not then in the least doubt the strict and literal truth of every word in the Bible, I soon persuaded myself that our Creed must be fully accepted.

Considering how fiercely I have been attacked by the orthodox, it seems ludicrous that I once intended to be a clergyman. Nor was this intention and my father's wish ever formerly given up, but died a natural death when, on leaving Cambridge, I joined the "Beagle" as naturalist. If the phrenologists are to be trusted, I was well fitted in one respect to be a clergyman. A few years ago the secretaries of a German psychological society asked me earnestly by letter for a photograph of myself; and some time afterwards I received the proceedings of one of the meetings, in which it seemed that the shape of my head had been the subject of a public discussion, and one of the speakers declared that I had the bump of reverence developed enough for ten priests.

As it was decided that I should be a clergyman, it was necessary that I should go to one of the English universities and take a degree; but as I had never opened a classical book since leaving school, I found to my dismay, that in the two intervening years I had actually forgotten, incredible as it may appear, almost everything which I had learnt, even to some few of the Greek letters. I did not therefore proceed to Cambridge at the usual time in October, but worked with a private tutor in Shrewsbury, and went to Cambridge after the Christmas vacation, early in 1828. I soon recovered my school standard of knowledge, and could translate easy Greek books, such as Homer and the Greek Testament, with moderate facility.

During the three years which I spent at Cambridge my time was wasted, as far as the academ-

ical studies were concerned, as completely as at
Edinburgh and at school. I attempted mathematics, and even went during the summer of 1828
with a private tutor (a very dull man) to Barmouth,
but I got on very slowly. The work was repugnant
to me, chiefly from my not being able to see any
meaning in the early steps in algebra. This impa-
tience was very foolish, and in after years I have
deeply regretted that I did not proceed far enough
at least to understand something of the great leading principles of mathematics, for men thus en-
dowed seem to have an extra sense. But I do not
believe that I should ever have succeeded beyond
a very low grade. With respect to Classics I did
nothing except attend a few compulsory college
lectures, and the attendance was almost nominal.
In my second year I had to work for a month or
two to pass the Little-Go, which I did easily. Again,
in my last year I worked with some earnestness
for my final degree of B.A., and brushed up my
Classics, together with a little Algebra and Euclid,
which latter gave me much pleasure, as it did at
school. In order to pass the B.A. examination, it
was also necessary to get up Paley's 'Evidences
of Christianity,' and his 'Moral Philosophy.' This
was done in a thorough manner, and I am convinced that I could have written out the whole

of the 'Evidences' with perfect correctness, but not of course in the clear language of Paley. The logic of this book and, as I may add, of his 'Natural Theology,' gave me as much delight as did Euclid. The careful study of these works, without attempting to learn any part by rote, was the only part of the academical course which, as I then felt and as I still believe, was of the least use to me in the education of my mind. I did not at that time trouble myself about Paley's premises; and taking these on trust, I was charmed and convinced by the long line of argumentation. By answering well the examination questions in Paley, by doing Euclid well, and by not failing miserably in Classics, I gained a good place among the oi polloi or crowd of men who do not go in for honours. Oddly enough, I cannot remember how high I stood, and my memory fluctuates between the fifth, tenth, or twelfth, name on the list. (Tenth in the list of January 1831.)

Public lectures on several branches were given in the University, attendance being quite voluntary; but I was so sickened with lectures at Edinburgh that I did not even attend Sedgwick's eloquent and interesting lectures. Had I done so I should probably have become a geologist earlier than I did. I attended, however, Henslow's lectures on Botany, and liked them much for their extreme clearness, and the admirable illustrations; but I did not study botany. Henslow used to take his pupils, including several of the older members of the University, field excursions, on foot or in coaches, to distant places, or in a barge down the river, and lectured on the rarer plants and animals which were observed. These excursions were delightful.

Although, as we shall presently see, there were some redeeming features in my life at Cambridge, my time was sadly wasted there, and worse than wasted. From my passion for shooting and for hunting, and, when this failed, for riding across country, I got into a sporting set, including some dissipated low-minded young men. We used often to dine together in the evening, though these dinners often included men of a higher stamp, and we sometimes drank too much, with jolly singing and playing at cards afterwards. I know that I ought to feel ashamed of days and evenings thus spent, but as some of my friends were very pleasant, and we were all in the highest spirits, I cannot help looking back to these times with much pleasure.

But I am glad to think that I had many other friends of a widely different nature. I was very intimate with Whitley (Rev. C. Whitley, Hon. Canon of Durham, formerly Reader in Natural Philosophy in Durham University.), who was afterwards Senior Wrangler, and we used continually to take long walks together. He inoculated me with a taste for pictures and good engravings, of which I bought some. I frequently went to the Fitzwilliam Gallery, and my taste must have been fairly good, for I certainly admired the best pictures, which I discussed with the old curator. I read also with much interest Sir Joshua Reynolds' book. This taste, though not natural to me, lasted for several years, and many of the pictures in the National Gallery in London gave me much pleasure; that of Sebastian del Piombo exciting in me a sense of sublimity.

I also got into a musical set, I believe by means of my warm-hearted friend, Herbert (The late John Maurice Herbert, County Court Judge of Cardiff and the Monmouth Circuit.), who took a high wrangler's degree. From associating with these men, and hearing them play, I acquired a strong taste for music, and used very often to time my walks so as to hear on week days the anthem in King's College Chapel. This gave me intense pleasure, so that my backbone would sometimes shiver. I am sure that there was no affectation or mere imitation in this taste, for I used generally to go by myself to King's College, and I sometimes hired the chorister boys to sing in my rooms. Nevertheless I am so utterly destitute of an ear, that I cannot perceive a discord, or keep time and hum a tune correctly; and it is a mystery how I could possibly have derived pleasure from music.

My musical friends soon perceived my state, and sometimes amused themselves by making me pass an examination, which consisted in ascertaining how many tunes I could recognise when they were played rather more quickly or slowly than usual. 'God save the King,' when thus played, was a sore puzzle. There was another man with almost as bad an ear as I had, and strange to say he played a little on the flute. Once I had the triumph of beating him in one of our musical examinations.

But no pursuit at Cambridge was followed with nearly so much eagerness or gave me so much pleasure as collecting beetles. It was the mere passion for collecting, for I did not dissect them, and rarely compared their external characters with published descriptions, but got them named anyhow. I will give a proof of my zeal: one day, on tearing off some old bark, I saw two rare beetles, and seized one in each hand; then I saw a third and new kind, which I could not bear to lose, so that I popped the one which I held in my right hand into my mouth. Alas! it ejected some intensely acrid fluid, which burnt my tongue so that I was forced to spit the beetle out, which was lost, as was the third one.

I was very successful in collecting, and invented two new methods; I employed a labourer to scrape during the winter, moss off old trees and place it in a large bag, and likewise to collect the rubbish at the bottom of the barges in which reeds are brought from the fens, and thus I got some very rare species. No poet ever felt more delighted at seeing his first poem published than I did at seeing, in Stephens' 'Illustrations of British Insects,' the magic words, "captured by C. Darwin, Esq." I was introduced to entomology by my second cousin W. Darwin Fox, a clever and most pleasant man, who was then at Christ's College, and with whom I became extremely intimate. Afterwards I became well acquainted, and went out collecting, with Albert Way of Trinity, who in after years became a well-known archaeologist; also with H. Thompson of the same College, afterwards a leading agriculturist, chairman of a great railway, and Member of Parliament. It seems therefore that a taste for collecting beetles is some indication of future success in life!

I am surprised what an indelible impression many of the beetles which I caught at Cambridge have left on my mind. I can remember the exact appearance of certain posts, old trees and banks where I made a good capture. The pretty Panagaeus crux-major was a treasure in those days, and here at Down I saw a beetle running across a walk, and on picking it up instantly perceived that it differed slightly from P. crux-major, and it turned out to be P. quadripunctatus, which is only a variety or closely allied species, differing from it very slightly in outline. I had never seen in those old days Licinus alive, which to an uneducated eye hardly differs from many of the black Carabidous beetles; but my sons found here a specimen, and I instantly recognised that it was new to me; yet I had not looked at a British beetle for the last twenty years.

I have not as yet mentioned a circumstance which influenced my whole career more than any other. This was my friendship with Professor Henslow. Before coming up to Cambridge, I had heard of him from my brother as a man who knew every branch of science, and I was accordingly prepared to reverence him. He kept open house once every week when all undergraduates, and some older members of the University, who were attached to science, used to meet in the evening. I soon got, through Fox, an invitation, and went there regularly. Before long I became well acquainted with Henslow, and during the latter half of my time at Cambridge took long walks with him on most days; so that I was called by some of the dons "the man who walks with Henslow;" and in the evening I was very often asked to join his family dinner. His knowledge was great in botany, entomology, chemistry, mineralogy, and geology. His strongest taste was to draw conclusions from long-continued minute observations. His judgment was excellent, and his whole mind well balanced; but I do not suppose that any one would say that he possessed much original genius. He was deeply religious, and so orthodox that he told me one day he should be grieved if a single word of the Thirty-nine Articles were altered. His moral qualities were in every way admirable. He was free from every tinge of vanity or other petty feeling; and I never saw a man who thought so little about himself or his own concerns. His temper was imperturbably good, with the most winning and courteous manners; yet, as I have seen, he could be roused by any bad action to the warmest indignation and prompt action.

I once saw in his company in the streets of Cambridge almost as horrid a scene as could have been witnessed during the French Revolution. Two body-snatchers had been arrested, and whilst being taken to prison had been torn from the constable by a crowd of the roughest men, who dragged them by their legs along the muddy and stony road. They were covered from head to foot with mud, and their faces were bleeding either from having been kicked or from the stones; they looked like corpses, but the crowd was so dense that I got only a few momentary glimpses of the wretched creatures. Never in my life have I seen such wrath painted on a man's face as was shown by Henslow at this horrid scene. He tried repeatedly to penetrate the mob; but it was simply impossible. He then rushed away to the mayor, telling me not to follow him, but to get more policemen. I forget the issue, except that the two men were got into the prison without being killed.

Henslow's benevolence was unbounded, as he proved by his many excellent schemes for his poor parishioners, when in after years he held the living of Hitcham. My intimacy with such a man ought to have been, and I hope was, an inestimable benefit. I cannot resist mentioning a trifling incident, which showed his kind consideration. Whilst examining some pollen-grains on a damp surface, I saw the tubes exserted, and instantly rushed off to communicate my surprising discovery to him. Now I do not suppose any other professor of botany could have helped laughing at my coming in such a hurry to make such a communication. But he agreed how interesting the phenomenon was, and explained its meaning, but made me clearly understand how well it was known; so I left him not in the least mortified, but well pleased at having discovered for myself so remarkable a fact, but determined not to be in such a hurry again to communicate my discoveries.

Dr. Whewell was one of the older and distinguished men who sometimes visited Henslow, and on several occasions I walked home with him at night. Next to Sir J. Mackintosh he was the best converser on grave subjects to whom I ever listened. Leonard Jenyns (The well-known Soame Jenyns was cousin to Mr. Jenyns' father.), who afterwards published some good essays in Natural History (Mr. Jenyns (now Blomefield) described the fish for the Zoology of the "Beagle"; and is author of a long series of papers, chiefly Zoological.), often stayed with Henslow, who was his brother-in-law. I visited him at his parsonage on the borders of the Fens [Swaffham Bulbeck], and had many a good walk and talk with him about Natural History. I became also acquainted with several other men older than me, who did not care much about science, but were friends of Henslow. One was a Scotchman, brother of Sir Alexander Ramsay, and tutor of Jesus College: he was a delightful man, but did not live for many years. Another was Mr. Dawes, afterwards Dean of Hereford, and famous for his success in the education of the poor. These men and others of the same standing, together with Henslow, used sometimes to take distant excursions into the country, which I was allowed to join, and they were most agreeable.

Looking back, I infer that there must have been something in me a little superior to the common run of youths, otherwise the above-mentioned men, so much older than me and higher in academical position, would never have allowed me to associate with them. Certainly I was not aware of any such superiority, and I remember one of my sporting friends, Turner, who saw me at work with my beetles, saying that I should some day be a Fellow of the Royal Society, and the notion seemed to me preposterous.

During my last year at Cambridge, I read with care and profound interest Humboldt's 'Personal Narrative.' This work, and Sir J. Herschel's 'Introduction to the Study of Natural Philosophy,' stirred up in me a burning zeal to add even the most humble contribution to the noble structure of Natural Science. No one or a dozen other books influenced me nearly so much as these two. I copied out from Humboldt long passages about Teneriffe, and read them aloud on one of the above-mentioned excursions, to (I think) Henslow, Ramsay, and Dawes, for on a previous occasion I had talked about the glories of Teneriffe, and some of the party declared they would endeavour to go there; but I think that they were only half in earnest. I was, however, quite in earnest, and got an introduction to a merchant in London to enquire about ships; but the scheme was, of course, knocked on the head by the voyage of the "Beagle".

My summer vacations were given up to collecting beetles, to some reading, and short tours. In the autumn my whole time was devoted to shooting, chiefly at Woodhouse and Maer, and sometimes with young Eyton of Eyton. Upon the whole the three years which I spent at Cambridge were the most joyful in my happy life; for I was then in excellent health, and almost always in high spirits.

As I had at first come up to Cambridge at Christmas, I was forced to keep two terms after passing my final examination, at the commencement of 1831; and Henslow then persuaded me to begin the study of geology. Therefore on my return to Shropshire I examined sections, and coloured a map of parts round Shrewsbury. Professor Sedgwick intended to visit North Wales in the beginning of August to pursue his famous geological investigations amongst the older rocks, and Henslow asked him to allow me to accompany him. (In connection with this tour my father used to tell a story about Sedgwick: they had started from their inn one morning, and had walked a mile or two, when Sedgwick suddenly stopped, and vowed that he would return, being certain "that damned scoundrel" (the waiter) had not given the chambermaid the sixpence intrusted to him for the purpose. He was ultimately persuaded to give up the project, seeing that there was no reason for suspecting the waiter of especial perfidy.— F.D.) Accordingly he came and slept at my father's house.

A short conversation with him during this evening produced a strong impression on my mind. Whilst examining an old gravel-pit near Shrewsbury, a labourer told me that he had found in it a large worn tropical Volute shell, such as may be seen on the chimney-pieces of cottages; and as he would not sell the shell, I was convinced that he had really found it in the pit. I told Sedgwick of the fact, and he at once said (no doubt truly) that it must have been thrown away by some one into the pit; but then added, if really embedded there it would be the greatest misfortune to geology, as it would overthrow all that we know about the superficial deposits of the Midland Counties. These gravel-beds belong in fact to the glacial period, and in after years I found in them broken arctic shells. But I was then utterly astonished at Sedgwick not being delighted at so wonderful a fact as a tropical shell being found near the surface in the middle of England. Nothing before had ever made me thoroughly realise, though I had read various scientific books, that science consists in grouping facts so that general laws or conclusions may be drawn from them.

Next morning we started for Llangollen, Conway, Bangor, and Capel Curig. This tour was of decided use in teaching me a little how to make out the geology of a country. Sedgwick often sent me on a line parallel to his, telling me to bring back specimens of the rocks and to mark the stratification on a map. I have little doubt that he did this for my good, as I was too ignorant to have aided him. On this tour I had a striking instance of how easy it is to overlook phenomena, however conspicuous, before they have been observed by any one. We spent many hours in Cwm Idwal, examining all the rocks with extreme care, as Sedgwick was anxious to find fossils in them; but neither of us saw a trace of the wonderful glacial phenomena all around us; we did not notice the plainly scored rocks, the perched boulders, the lateral and terminal moraines. Yet these phenomena are so conspicuous that, as I declared in a paper published many years afterwards in the 'Philosophical Magazine' ('Philosophical Magazine,' 1842.), a house burnt down by fire did not tell its story more plainly than did this valley. If it had still been filled by a glacier, the phenomena would have been less distinct than they now are.

At Capel Curig I left Sedgwick and went in a straight line by compass and map across the mountains to Barmouth, never following any track unless it coincided with my course. I thus came on some strange wild places, and enjoyed much this manner of travelling. I visited Barmouth to see some Cambridge friends who were reading there, and thence returned to Shrewsbury and to Maer for shooting; for at that time I should have thought myself mad to give up the first days of partridge-shooting for geology or any other science.

"Voyage Of The 'Beagle' From December 27, 1831, To October 2, 1836."

On returning home from my short geological tour in North Wales, I found a letter from Henslow, informing me that Captain Fitz-Roy was willing to give up part of his own cabin to any young man who would volunteer to go with him without pay as naturalist to the Voyage of the "Beagle". I have given, as I believe, in my MS. Journal an account of all the circumstances which then occurred; I will here only say that I was instantly eager to accept the offer, but my father strongly objected, adding the words, fortunate for me, "If you can find any man of common sense who advises you to go I will give my consent." So I wrote that evening and refused the offer. On the next morning I went to Maer to be ready for September 1st, and, whilst out shooting, my uncle (Josiah Wedgwood.) sent for me, offering to drive me over to Shrewsbury and talk with my father, as my uncle thought it would be wise in me to accept the offer. My father always maintained that he was one of the most sensible men in the world, and he at once consented in the kindest manner. I had been rather extravagant at Cambridge, and to console my father, said, "that I should be deuced clever to spend more than my allowance whilst on board the 'Beagle';" but he answered with a smile, "But they tell me you are very clever."

Next day I started for Cambridge to see Henslow, and thence to London to see Fitz-Roy, and all was soon arranged. Afterwards, on becoming very intimate with Fitz-Roy, I heard that I had run a very narrow risk of being rejected, on account of the shape of my nose! He was an ardent disciple of Lavater, and was convinced that he could judge of a man's character by the outline of his features; and he doubted whether any one with my nose could possess sufficient energy and determination for the voyage. But I think he was afterwards well satisfied that my nose had spoken falsely.

Fitz-Roy's character was a singular one, with very many noble features: he was devoted to his duty, generous to a fault, bold, determined, and indomitably energetic, and an ardent friend to all under his sway. He would undertake any sort of trouble to assist those whom he thought deserved assistance. He was a handsome man, strikingly like a gentleman, with highly courteous manners, which resembled those of his maternal uncle, the famous Lord Castlereagh, as I was told by the Minister at Rio. Nevertheless he must have inherited much in his appearance from Charles II., for Dr. Wallich gave me a collection of photographs which he had made, and I was struck with the resemblance of one to Fitz-Roy; and on looking at the name, I found it Ch. E. Sobieski Stuart, Count d'Albanie, a descendant of the same monarch.

Fitz-Roy's temper was a most unfortunate one. It was usually worst in the early morning, and with his eagle eye he could generally detect something amiss about the ship, and was then unsparing in his blame. He was very kind to me, but was a man very difficult to live with on the intimate terms which necessarily followed from our messing by ourselves in the same cabin. We had several quarrels; for instance, early in the voyage at Bahia, in Brazil, he defended and praised slavery, which I abominated, and told me that he had just visited a great slave-owner, who had called up many of his slaves and asked them whether they were happy, and whether they wished to be free, and all answered "No." I then asked him, perhaps with a sneer, whether he thought that the answer of slaves in the presence of their master was worth anything? This made him excessively angry, and he said that as I doubted his word we could not live any longer together. I thought that I should have been compelled to leave the ship; but as soon as the news spread, which it did quickly, as the captain sent for the first lieutenant to assuage his anger by abusing me, I was deeply gratified by receiving an invitation from all the gun-room officers to mess with them. But after a few hours Fitz-Roy showed his usual magnanimity by sending an officer to me with an apology and a request that I would continue to live with him.

His character was in several respects one of the most noble which I have ever known.

The voyage of the "Beagle" has been by far the most important event in my life, and has determined my whole career; yet it depended on so small a circumstance as my uncle offering to drive me thirty miles to Shrewsbury, which few uncles would have done, and on such a trifle as the shape of my nose. I have always felt that I owe to the voyage the first real training or education of my mind; I was led to attend closely to several branches of natural history, and thus my powers of observation were improved, though they were always fairly developed.

The investigation of the geology of all the places visited was far more important, as reasoning here comes into play. On first examining a new district nothing can appear more hopeless than the chaos of rocks; but by recording the stratification and nature of the rocks and fossils at many points, always reasoning and predicting what will be found elsewhere, light soon begins to dawn on the district, and the structure of the whole becomes more or less intelligible. I had brought with me the first volume of Lyell's 'Principles of Geology,' which I studied attentively; and the book was of the highest service to me in many ways. The very first place which I examined, namely St. Jago in the Cape de Verde islands, showed me clearly the wonderful superiority of Lyell's manner of treating geology, compared with that of any other author, whose works I had with me or ever afterwards read.

Another of my occupations was collecting animals of all classes, briefly describing and roughly dissecting many of the marine ones; but from not being able to draw, and from not having sufficient anatomical knowledge, a great pile of MS. which I made during the voyage has proved almost useless. I thus lost much time, with the exception of that spent in acquiring some knowledge of the Crustaceans, as this was of service when in after years I undertook a monograph of the Cirripedia.

During some part of the day I wrote my Journal, and took much pains in describing carefully and vividly all that I had seen; and this was good practice. My Journal served also, in part, as letters to my home, and portions were sent to England whenever there was an opportunity.

The above various special studies were, however, of no importance compared with the habit of energetic industry and of concentrated attention to whatever I was engaged in, which I then acquired. Everything about which I thought or read was made to bear directly on what I had seen or was likely to see; and this habit of mind was continued during the five years of the voyage. I feel sure that it was this training which has enabled me to do whatever I have done in science.

Looking backwards, I can now perceive how my love for science gradually preponderated over every other taste. During the first two years my old passion for shooting survived in nearly full force, and I shot myself all the birds and animals for my collection; but gradually I gave up my gun more and more, and finally altogether, to my servant, as shooting interfered with my work, more especially with making out the geological structure of a country. I discovered, though unconsciously and insensibly, that the pleasure of observing and reasoning was a much higher one than that of skill and sport. That my mind became developed through my pursuits during the voyage is rendered probable by a remark made by my father, who was the most acute observer whom I ever saw, of a sceptical disposition, and far from being a believer in phrenology; for on first seeing me after the voyage, he turned round to my sisters, and exclaimed, "Why, the shape of his head is quite altered."

To return to the voyage. On September 11th (1831), I paid a flying visit with Fitz-Roy to the "Beagle" at Plymouth. Thence to Shrewsbury to wish my father and sisters a long farewell. On October 24th I took up my residence at Plymouth, and remained there until December 27th, when the "Beagle" finally left the shores of England for her circumnavigation of the world. We made two earlier attempts to sail, but were driven back each time by heavy gales. These two months at Plymouth were the most miserable which I ever spent, though I exerted myself in various ways. I was out of spirits at the thought of leaving all my family and friends for so long a time, and the weather seemed to me inexpressibly gloomy. I was also troubled with palpitation and pain about the heart, and like many a young ignorant man, especially one with a smattering of medical knowledge, was convinced that I had heart disease. I did not consult any doctor, as I fully expected to hear the verdict that I was not fit for the voyage, and I was resolved to go at all hazards.

I need not here refer to the events of the voyage—where we went and what we did—as I have given a sufficiently full account in my published Journal. The glories of the vegetation of the Tropics rise before my mind at the present time more vividly than anything else; though the sense of sublimity, which the great deserts of Patagonia and the forest-clad mountains of Tierra del Fuego excited in me, has left an indelible impression on my mind. The sight of a naked savage in his native land is an event which can never be forgotten. Many of my excursions on horseback through wild countries, or in the boats, some of which lasted several weeks, were deeply interesting: their discomfort and some degree of danger were at that time hardly a drawback, and none at all afterwards. I also reflect with high satisfaction on some of my scientific work, such as solving the problem of coral islands, and making out the geological structure of certain islands, for instance, St. Helena. Nor must I pass over the discovery of the singular relations of the animals and plants inhabiting the several islands of the Galapagos archipelago, and of all of them to the inhabitants of South America.

As far as I can judge of myself, I worked to the utmost during the voyage from the mere pleasure of investigation, and from my strong desire to add a few facts to the great mass of facts in Natural Science. But I was also ambitious to take a fair place among scientific men,—whether more ambitious or less so than most of my fellow-workers, I can form no opinion.

The geology of St. Jago is very striking, yet simple: a stream of lava formerly flowed over the bed of the sea, formed of triturated recent shells and corals, which it has baked into a hard white rock. Since then the whole island has been upheaved. But the line of white rock revealed to me a new and important fact, namely, that there had been afterwards subsidence round the craters, which had since been in action, and had poured forth lava. It then first dawned on me that I might perhaps write a book on the geology of the various countries visited, and this made me thrill with delight. That was a memorable hour to me, and how distinctly I can call to mind the low cliff of lava beneath which I rested, with the sun glaring hot, a few strange desert plants growing near, and with living corals in the tidal pools at my feet. Later in the voyage, Fitz-Roy asked me to read some of my Journal, and declared it would be worth publishing; so here was a second book in prospect!

Towards the close of our voyage I received a letter whilst at Ascension, in which my sisters told me that Sedgwick had called on my father, and said that I should take a place among the leading scientific men. I could not at the time understand how he could have learnt anything of my proceedings, but I heard (I believe afterwards) that Henslow had read some of the letters which I wrote to him before the Philosophical Society of Cambridge (Read at the meeting held November 16, 1835, and printed in a pamphlet of 31 pages for distribution among the members of the Society.), and had printed them for private distribution. My collection of fossil bones, which had been sent to Henslow, also excited considerable attention amongst palaeontologists. After reading this letter, I clambered over the mountains of Ascension with a bounding step, and made the volcanic rocks resound under my geological hammer. All this shows how ambitious I was; but I think that I can say with truth that in after years, though I cared in the highest degree for the approbation of such men as Lyell and Hooker, who were my friends, I did not care much about the general public. I do not mean to say that a favourable review or a large sale of my books did not please me greatly, but the pleasure was a fleeting one, and I am sure that I have never turned one inch out of my course to gain fame.

From My Return To England (October 2, 1836) To My Marriage (January 29, 1839.)

These two years and three months were the most active ones which I ever spent, though I was occasionally unwell, and so lost some time. After going backwards and forwards several times between Shrewsbury, Maer, Cambridge, and London, I settled in lodgings at Cambridge (In Fitzwilliam Street.) on December 13th, where all my collections were under the care of Henslow. I stayed here three months, and got my minerals and rocks examined by the aid of Professor Miller.

I began preparing my 'Journal of Travels,' which was not hard work, as my MS. Journal had been written with care, and my chief labour was making an abstract of my more interesting scientific results. I sent also, at the request of Lyell, a short account of my observations on the elevation of the coast of Chile to the Geological Society. ('Geolog. Soc. Proc. ii. 1838, pages 446-449.)

On March 7th, 1837, I took lodgings in Great Marlborough Street in London, and remained there for nearly two years, until I was married. During these two years I finished my Journal, read several papers before the Geological Society, began preparing the MS. for my 'Geological Observations,' and arranged for the publication of the 'Zoology of the Voyage of the "Beagle".' In July I opened my first note-book for facts in relation to the Origin of Species, about which I had long reflected, and never ceased working for the next twenty years.

During these two years I also went a little into society, and acted as one of the honorary secretaries of the Geological Society. I saw a great deal of Lyell. One of his chief characteristics was his sympathy with the work of others, and I was as much astonished as delighted at the interest which he showed when, on my return to England, I explained to him my views on coral reefs. This encouraged me greatly, and his advice and example had much influence on me. During this time I saw also a good deal of Robert Brown; I used often to call and sit with him during his breakfast on Sunday mornings, and he poured forth a rich treasure of curious observations and acute remarks, but they almost always related to minute points, and he never with me discussed large or general questions in science.

During these two years I took several short excursions as a relaxation, and one longer one to the Parallel Roads of Glen Roy, an account of which was published in the 'Philosophical Transactions.' (1839, pages 39-82.) This paper was a great failure, and I am ashamed of it. Having been deeply impressed with what I had seen of the elevation of the land of South America, I attributed the parallel lines to the action of the sea; but I had to give up this view when Agassiz propounded his glacier-lake theory. Because no other explanation was possible under our then state of knowledge, I argued in favour of sea-action; and my error has been a good lesson to me never to trust in science to the principle of exclusion.

As I was not able to work all day at science, I read a good deal during these two years on various subjects, including some metaphysical books; but I was not well fitted for such studies. About this time I took much delight in Wordsworth's and Coleridge's poetry; and can boast that I read the 'Excursion' twice through. Formerly Milton's 'Paradise Lost' had been my chief favourite, and in my excursions during the voyage of the "Beagle", when I could take only a single volume, I always chose Milton.

From My Marriage, January 29, 1839, And Residence In Upper Gower Street To Our Leaving London And Settling At Down, September 14, 1842

(After speaking of his happy married life, and of his children, he continues:—)

During the three years and eight months whilst we resided in London, I did less scientific work, though I worked as hard as I possibly could, than during any other equal length of time in my life. This was owing to frequently recurring unwellness, and to one long and serious illness. The greater part of my time, when I could do anything, was devoted to my work on 'Coral Reefs,' which I had begun before my marriage, and of which the last proof-sheet was corrected on May 6th, 1842. This book, though a small one, cost me twenty months of hard work, as I had to read every work on the islands of the Pacific and to consult many charts. It was thought highly of by scientific men, and the theory therein given is, I think, now well established.

No other work of mine was begun in so deductive a spirit as this, for the whole theory was thought out on the west coast of South America, before I had seen a true coral reef. I had therefore only to verify and extend my views by a careful examination of living reefs. But it should be observed that I had during the two previous years been incessantly attending to the effects on the shores of South America of the intermittent elevation of the land, together with denudation and the deposition of sediment. This necessarily led me to reflect much on the effects of subsidence, and it was easy to replace in imagination the continued deposition of sediment by the upward growth of corals. To do this was to form my theory of the formation of barrier-reefs and atolls.

Besides my work on coral-reefs, during my residence in London, I read before the Geological Society papers on the Erratic Boulders of South America ('Geolog. Soc. Proc.' iii. 1842.), on Earthquakes ('Geolog. Trans. v. 1840.), and on the Formation by the Agency of Earth-worms of Mould. ('Geolog. Soc. Proc. ii. 1838.) I also continued to superintend the publication of the 'Zoology of the Voyage of the "Beagle".' Nor did I ever intermit collecting facts bearing on the origin of species; and I could sometimes do this when I could do nothing else from illness.

In the summer of 1842 I was stronger than I had been for some time, and took a little tour by myself in North Wales, for the sake of observing the effects of the old glaciers which formerly filled all the larger valleys. I published a short account of what I saw in the 'Philosophical Magazine.' ('Philosophical Magazine,' 1842.) This excursion interested me greatly, and it was the last time I was ever strong enough to climb mountains or to take long walks such as are necessary for geological work.

During the early part of our life in London, I was strong enough to go into general society, and saw a good deal of several scientific men, and other more or less distinguished men. I will give my impressions with respect to some of them, though I have little to say worth saying.

I saw more of Lyell than of any other man, both before and after my marriage. His mind was characterised, as it appeared to me, by clearness, caution, sound judgment, and a good deal of originality. When I made any remark to him on Geology, he never rested until he saw the whole case clearly, and often made me see it more clearly than I had done before. He would advance all possible objections to my suggestion, and even after these were exhausted would long remain dubious.

A second characteristic was his hearty sympathy with the work of other scientific men. (The slight repetition here observable is accounted for by the notes on Lyell, etc., having been added in April, 1881, a few years after the rest of the 'Recollections' were written.)

On my return from the voyage of the "Beagle", I explained to him my views on coral-reefs, which differed from his, and I was greatly surprised and encouraged by the vivid interest which he showed. His delight in science was ardent, and he felt the keenest interest in the future progress of mankind. He was very kind-hearted, and thoroughly liberal in his religious beliefs, or rather disbeliefs; but he was a strong theist. His candour was highly remarkable. He exhibited this by becoming a convert to the Descent theory, though he had gained much fame by opposing Lamarck's views, and this after he had grown old. He reminded me that I had many years before said to him, when discussing the opposition of the old school of geologists to his new views, "What a good thing it would be if every scientific man was to die when sixty years old, as afterwards he would be sure to oppose all new doctrines." But he hoped that now he might be allowed to live.

The science of Geology is enormously indebted

to Lyell—more so, as I believe, than to any other man who ever lived. When [I was] starting on the voyage of the "Beagle", the sagacious Henslow, who, like all other geologists, believed at that time in successive cataclysms, advised me to get and study the first volume of the 'Principles,' which had then just been published, but on no account to accept the views therein advocated. How differently would anyone now speak of the 'Principles'! I am proud to remember that the first place, namely, St. Jago, in the Cape de Verde archipelago, in which I geologised, convinced me of the infinite superiority of Lyell's views over those advocated in any other work known to me.

The powerful effects of Lyell's works could formerly be plainly seen in the different progress of the science in France and England. The present total oblivion of Elie de Beaumont's wild hypotheses, such as his 'Craters of Elevation' and 'Lines of Elevation' (which latter hypothesis I heard Sedgwick at the Geological Society lauding to the skies), may be largely attributed to Lyell.

I saw a good deal of Robert Brown, "facile Princeps Botanicorum," as he was called by Humboldt. He seemed to me to be chiefly remarkable for the minuteness of his observations, and their perfect accuracy. His knowledge was extraordinarily great, and much died with him, owing to his excessive fear of ever making a mistake. He poured out his knowledge to me in the most unreserved manner, yet was strangely jealous on some points. I called on him two or three times before the voyage of the "Beagle", and on one occasion he asked me to look through a microscope and describe what I saw. This I did, and believe now that it was the marvellous currents of protoplasm in some vegetable cell. I then asked him what I had seen; but he answered me, "That is my little secret."

He was capable of the most generous actions. When old, much out of health, and quite unfit for any exertion, he daily visited (as Hooker told me) an old man-servant, who lived at a distance (and whom he supported), and read aloud to him. This is enough to make up for any degree of scientific penuriousness or jealousy.

I may here mention a few other eminent men, whom I have occasionally seen, but I have little to say about them worth saying. I felt a high reverence for Sir J. Herschel, and was delighted to dine with him at his charming house at the Cape of Good Hope, and afterwards at his London house. I saw him, also, on a few other occasions. He never talked much, but every word which he uttered was worth listening to.

I once met at breakfast at Sir R. Murchison's house the illustrious Humboldt, who honoured me by expressing a wish to see me. I was a little disappointed with the great man, but my antici-pations probably were too high. I can remember nothing distinctly about our interview, except that Humboldt was very cheerful and talked much.

—reminds me of Buckle whom I once met at Hensleigh Wedgwood's. I was very glad to learn from him his system of collecting facts. He told me that he bought all the books which he read, and made a full index, to each, of the facts which he thought might prove serviceable to him, and that he could always remember in what book he had read anything, for his memory was wonder-ful. I asked him how at first he could judge what facts would be serviceable, and he answered that he did not know, but that a sort of instinct guided him. From this habit of making indices, he was enabled to give the astonishing number of refer-ences on all sorts of subjects, which may be found in his 'History of Civilisation.' This book I thought most interesting, and read it twice, but I doubt whether his generalisations are worth anything. Buckle was a great talker, and I listened to him saying hardly a word, nor indeed could I have done so for he left no gaps. When Mrs. Farrer began to sing, I jumped up and said that I must listen to her; after I had moved away he turned around to a friend and said (as was overheard by my brother), "Well, Mr. Darwin's books are much better than his conversation."

Of other great literary men, I once met Sydney Smith at Dean Milman's house. There was something inexplicably amusing in every word which he uttered. Perhaps this was partly due to the expectation of being amused. He was talking about Lady Cork, who was then extremely old. This was the lady who, as he said, was once so much affected by one of his charity sermons, that she *borrowed* a guinea from a friend to put in the plate. He now said "It is generally believed that my dear old friend Lady Cork has been overlooked," and he said this in such a manner that no one could for a moment doubt that he meant that his dear old friend had been overlooked by the devil. How he managed to express this I know not.

I likewise once met Macaulay at Lord Stanhope's (the historian's) house, and as there was only one other man at dinner, I had a grand opportunity of hearing him converse, and he was very agreeable. He did not talk at all too much; nor indeed could such a man talk too much, as long as he allowed others to turn the stream of his conversation, and this he did allow.

Lord Stanhope once gave me a curious little proof of the accuracy and fulness of Macaulay's memory: many historians used often to meet at Lord Stanhope's house, and in discussing various subjects they would sometimes differ from Macaulay, and formerly they often referred to some book to see who was right; but latterly, as Lord Stanhope noticed, no historian ever took this trouble, and whatever Macaulay said was final.

On another occasion I met at Lord Stanhope's house, one of his parties of historians and other literary men, and amongst them were Motley and Grote. After luncheon I walked about Chevening Park for nearly an hour with Grote, and was much interested by his conversation and pleased by the simplicity and absence of all pretension in his manners.

Long ago I dined occasionally with the old Earl, the father of the historian; he was a strange man, but what little I knew of him I liked much. He was frank, genial, and pleasant. He had strongly marked features, with a brown complexion, and his clothes, when I saw him, were all brown. He seemed to believe in everything which was to others utterly incredible. He said one day to me,

"Why don't you give up your fiddle-faddle of geology and zoology, and turn to the occult sciences!" The historian, then Lord Mahon, seemed shocked at such a speech to me, and his charming wife much amused.

The last man whom I will mention is Carlyle, seen by me several times at my brother's house, and two or three times at my own house. His talk was very racy and interesting, just like his writings, but he sometimes went on too long on the same subject. I remember a funny dinner at my brother's, where, amongst a few others, were Babbage and Lyell, both of whom liked to talk. Carlyle, however, silenced every one by haranguing during the whole dinner on the advantages of silence. After dinner Babbage, in his grimmest manner, thanked Carlyle for his very interesting lecture on silence.

Carlyle sneered at almost every one: one day in my house he called Grote's 'History' "a fetid quagmire, with nothing spiritual about it." I always thought, until his 'Reminiscences' appeared, that his sneers were partly jokes, but this now seems rather doubtful. His expression was that of a depressed, almost despondent yet benevolent man; and it is notorious how heartily he laughed. I believe that his benevolence was real, though stained by not a little jealousy. No one can doubt about his extraordinary power of drawing pictures of things and men—far more vivid, as it appears to me, than any drawn by Macaulay. Whether his pictures of men were true ones is another question.

He has been all-powerful in impressing some grand moral truths on the minds of men. On the other hand, his views about slavery were revolting. In his eyes might was right. His mind seemed to me a very narrow one; even if all branches of science, which he despised, are excluded. It is astonishing to me that Kingsley should have spoken of him as a man well fitted to advance science. He laughed to scorn the idea that a mathematician, such as Whewell, could judge, as I maintained he could, of Goethe's views on light. He thought it a most ridiculous thing that any one should care whether a glacier moved a little quicker or a little slower, or moved at all. As far as I could judge, I never met a man with a mind so ill adapted for scientific research.

Whilst living in London, I attended as regularly as I could the meetings of several scientific societies, and acted as secretary to the Geological Society. But such attendance, and ordinary society, suited my health so badly that we resolved to live in the country, which we both preferred and have never repented of.

Residence At Down From September 14, 1842, To The Present Time, 1876

After several fruitless searches in Surrey and else-where, we found this house and purchased it. I was pleased with the diversified appearance of vegetation proper to a chalk district, and so un-like what I had been accustomed to in the Midland counties; and still more pleased with the extreme quietness and rusticity of the place. It is not, how-ever, quite so retired a place as a writer in a Ger-man periodical makes it, who says that my house can be approached only by a mule-track! Our fixing ourselves here has answered admirably in one way, which we did not anticipate, namely, by being very convenient for frequent visits from our children.

Few persons can have lived a more retired life than we have done. Besides short visits to the houses of relations, and occasionally to the sea-side or elsewhere, we have gone nowhere. Dur-ing the first part of our residence we went a little into society, and received a few friends here; but my health almost always suffered from the excitement, violent shivering and vomiting attacks being thus brought on. I have therefore been compelled for many years to give up all dinner-parties; and this has been somewhat of a deprivation to me, as such parties always put me into high spirits. From the same cause I have been able to invite here very few scientific acquaintances.

My chief enjoyment and sole employment throughout life has been scientific work; and the excitement from such work makes me for the time forget, or drives quite away, my daily discomfort. I have therefore nothing to record during the rest of my life, except the publication of my several books. Perhaps a few details how they arose may be worth giving.

My Several Publications

In the early part of 1844, my observations on the volcanic islands visited during the voyage of the "Beagle" were published. In 1845, I took much pains in correcting a new edition of my 'Journal of Researches,' which was originally published in 1839 as part of Fitz-Roy's work. The success of this, my first literary child, always tickles my vanity more than that of any of my other books. Even to this day it sells steadily in England and the United States, and has been translated for the second time into German, and into French and other languages. This success of a book of travels, especially of a scientific one, so many years after its first publication, is surprising. Ten thousand copies have been sold in England of the second edition. In 1846 my 'Geological Observations on South America' were published. I record in a little diary, which I have always kept, that my three geological books ('Coral Reefs' included) consumed four and a half years' steady work; "and now it is ten years since my return to England. How much time have I lost by illness?" I have nothing to say about these three books except that to my surprise new editions have lately been called for. ('Geological Observations,' 2nd Edit.1876. 'Coral Reefs,' 2nd Edit. 1874.)

In October, 1846, I began to work on 'Cirripedia.' When on the coast of Chile, I found a most curious form, which burrowed into the shells of Concholepas, and which differed so much from all other Cirripedes that I had to form a new sub-order for its sole reception. Lately an allied burrowing genus has been found on the shores of Portugal. To understand the structure of my new Cirripede I had to examine and dissect many of the common forms; and this gradually led me on to take up the whole group. I worked steadily on this subject for the next eight years, and ultimately published two thick volumes (Published by the Ray Society.), describing all the known living species, and two thin quartos on the extinct species. I do not doubt that Sir E. Lytton Bulwer had me in his mind when he introduced in one of his novels a Professor Long, who had written two huge volumes on limpets.

Although I was employed during eight years on this work, yet I record in my diary that about two years out of this time was lost by illness. On this account I went in 1848 for some months to Malvern for hydropathic treatment, which did me much good, so that on my return home I was able to resume work. So much was I out of health that when my dear father died on November 13th, 1848, I was unable to attend his funeral or to act as one of his executors.

My work on the Cirripedia possesses, I think, considerable value, as besides describing several new and remarkable forms, I made out the homologies of the various parts—I discovered the cementing apparatus, though I blundered dreadfully about the cement glands—and lastly I proved the existence in certain genera of minute males complemental to and parasitic on the hermaphrodites. This latter discovery has at last been fully confirmed; though at one time a German writer was pleased to attribute the whole account to my fertile imagination. The Cirripedes form a highly varying and difficult group of species to class; and my work was of considerable use to me, when I had to discuss in the 'Origin of Species' the principles of a natural classification. Nevertheless, I doubt whether the work was worth the consumption of so much time.

From September 1854 I devoted my whole time to arranging my huge pile of notes, to observing, and to experimenting in relation to the transmutation of species. During the voyage of the "Beagle" I had been deeply impressed by discovering in the Pampean formation great fossil animals covered with armour like that on the existing armadillos; secondly, by the manner in which closely allied animals replace one another in proceeding southwards over the Continent; and thirdly, by the South American character of most of the productions of the Galapagos archipelago, and more especially by the manner in which they differ slightly on each island of the group; none of the islands appearing to be very ancient in a geological sense.

It was evident that such facts as these, as well as many others, could only be explained on the supposition that species gradually become modified; and the subject haunted me. But it was equally evident that neither the action of the surrounding conditions, nor the will of the organisms (especially in the case of plants) could account for the innumerable cases in which organisms of every kind are beautifully adapted to their habits of life—for instance, a woodpecker or a tree-frog to climb trees, or a seed for dispersal by hooks or plumes. I had always been much struck by such adaptations, and until these could be explained it seemed to me almost useless to endeavour to prove by indirect evidence that species have been modified.

After my return to England it appeared to me that by following the example of Lyell in Geology, and by collecting all facts which bore in any way on the variation of animals and plants under domestication and nature, some light might perhaps be thrown on the whole subject. My first note-book was opened in July 1837. I worked on true Baconian principles, and without any theory collected facts on a wholesale scale, more especially with respect to domesticated productions, by printed enquiries, by conversation with skilful breeders and gardeners, and by extensive reading. When I see the list of books of all kinds which I read and abstracted, including whole series of Journals and Transactions, I am surprised at my industry. I soon perceived that selection was the keystone of man's success in making useful races of animals and plants. But how selection could be applied to organisms living in a state of nature remained for some time a mystery to me.

In October 1838, that is, fifteen months after I had begun my systematic enquiry, I happened to read for amusement 'Malthus on Population,' and being well prepared to appreciate the struggle for existence which everywhere goes on from long-continued observation of the habits of animals and plants, it at once struck me that under these circumstances favourable variations would tend to be preserved, and unfavourable ones to be destroyed. The result of this would be the formation of new species. Here then I had at last got a theory by which to work; but I was so anxious to avoid prejudice, that I determined not for some time to write even the briefest sketch of it. In June 1842 I first allowed myself the satisfaction of writing a very brief abstract of my theory in pencil in 35 pages; and this was enlarged during the summer of 1844 into one of 230 pages, which I had fairly copied out and still possess.

But at that time I overlooked one problem of great importance; and it is astonishing to me, except on the principle of Columbus and his egg, how I could have overlooked it and its solution. This problem is the tendency in organic beings descended from the same stock to diverge in character as they become modified. That they have diverged greatly is obvious from the manner in which species of all kinds can be classed under genera, genera under families, families under suborders and so forth; and I can remember the very spot in the road, whilst in my carriage, when to my joy the solution occurred to me; and this was long after I had come to Down. The solution, as I believe, is that the modified offspring of all dominant and increasing forms tend to become adapted to many and highly diversified places in the economy of nature.

Early in 1856 Lyell advised me to write out my views pretty fully, and I began at once to do so on a scale three or four times as extensive as that which was afterwards followed in my 'Origin of Species;' yet it was only an abstract of the materials which I had collected, and I got through about half the work on this scale. But my plans were overthrown, for early in the summer of 1858 Mr. Wallace, who was then in the Malay archipelago, sent me an essay "On the Tendency of Varieties to depart indefinitely from the Original Type;" and this essay contained exactly the same theory as mine. Mr. Wallace expressed the wish that if I thought well of his essay, I should sent it to Lyell for perusal.

The circumstances under which I consented at the request of Lyell and Hooker to allow of an abstract from my MS., together with a letter to Asa Gray, dated September 5, 1857, to be published at the same time with Wallace's Essay, are given in the 'Journal of the Proceedings of the Linnean Society,' 1858, page 45. I was at first very unwilling to consent, as I thought Mr. Wallace might consider my doing so unjustifiable, for I did not then know how generous and noble was his disposition. The extract from my MS. and the letter to Asa Gray had neither been intended for publication, and were badly written. Mr. Wallace's essay, on the other hand, was admirably expressed and quite clear. Nevertheless, our joint productions excited very little attention, and the only published notice of them which I can remember was by Professor Haughton of Dublin, whose verdict was that all that was new in them was false, and what was true was old. This shows how necessary it is that any new view should be explained at considerable length in order to arouse public attention.

In September 1858 I set to work by the strong advice of Lyell and Hooker to prepare a volume on the transmutation of species, but was often interrupted by ill-health, and short visits to Dr. Lane's delightful hydropathic establishment at Moor Park. I abstracted the MS. begun on a much larger scale in 1856, and completed the volume on the same reduced scale. It cost me thirteen months and ten days' hard labour. It was published under the title of the 'Origin of Species,' in November 1859. Though considerably added to and corrected in the later editions, it has remained substantially the same book.

It is no doubt the chief work of my life. It was from the first highly successful. The first small edition of 1250 copies was sold on the day of publication, and a second edition of 3000 copies soon afterwards. Sixteen thousand copies have now (1876) been sold in England; and considering how stiff a book it is, this is a large sale. It has been translated into almost every European tongue, even into such languages as Spanish, Bohemian, Polish, and Russian. It has also, according to Miss Bird, been translated into Japanese (Miss Bird is mistaken, as I learn from Prof. Mitsukuri.—F.D.), and is there much studied. Even an essay in Hebrew has appeared on it, showing that the theory is contained in the Old Testament! The reviews were very numerous; for some time I collected all that appeared on the 'Origin' and on my related books, and these amount (excluding newspaper reviews) to 265; but after a time I gave up the attempt in despair. Many separate essays and books on the subject have appeared; and in Germany a catalogue or bibliography on "Darwinismus" has appeared every year or two.

The success of the 'Origin' may, I think, be attributed in large part to my having long before written two condensed sketches, and to my having finally abstracted a much larger manuscript, which was itself an abstract. By this means I was enabled to select the more striking facts and conclusions. I had, also, during many years followed a golden rule, namely, that whenever a published fact, a new observation or thought came across me, which was opposed to my general results, to make a memorandum of it without fail and at once; for I had found by experience that such facts and thoughts were far more apt to escape from the memory than favourable ones. Owing to this habit, very few objections were raised against my views which I had not at least noticed and attempted to answer.

It has sometimes been said that the success of the 'Origin' proved "that the subject was in the air," or "that men's minds were prepared for it." I do not think that this is strictly true, for I occasionally sounded not a few naturalists, and never happened to come across a single one who seemed to doubt about the permanence of species. Even Lyell and Hooker, though they would listen with interest to me, never seemed to agree. I tried once or twice to explain to able men what I meant by Natural Selection, but signally failed. What I believe was strictly true is that innumerable well-observed facts were stored in the minds of naturalists ready to take their proper places as soon as any theory which would receive them was sufficiently explained. Another element in the success of the book was its moderate size; and this I owe to the appearance of Mr. Wallace's essay; had I published on the scale in which I began to write in 1856, the book would have been four or five times as large as the 'Origin,' and very few would have had the patience to read it.

I gained much by my delay in publishing from about 1839, when the theory was clearly conceived, to 1859; and I lost nothing by it, for I cared very little whether men attributed most originality to me or Wallace; and his essay no doubt aided in the reception of the theory. I was forestalled in only one important point, which my vanity has always made me regret, namely, the explanation by means of the Glacial period of the presence of the same species of plants and of some few animals on distant mountain summits and in the arctic regions. This view pleased me so much that I wrote it out in extenso, and I believe that it was read by Hooker some years before E. Forbes published his celebrated memoir ('Geolog. Survey Mem.,' 1846.) on the subject. In the very few points in which we differed, I still think that I was in the right. I have never, of course, alluded in print to my having independently worked out this view.

Hardly any point gave me so much satisfaction when I was at work on the 'Origin,' as the explanation of the wide difference in many classes between the embryo and the adult animal, and of the close resemblance of the embryos within the same class. No notice of this point was taken, as far as I remember, in the early reviews of the 'Origin,' and I recollect expressing my surprise on this head in a letter to Asa Gray. Within late years several reviewers have given the whole credit to Fritz Muller and Hackel, who undoubtedly have worked it out much more fully, and in some respects more correctly than I did. I had materials for a whole chapter on the subject, and I ought to have made the discussion longer; for it is clear that I failed to impress my readers; and he who succeeds in doing so deserves, in my opinion, all the credit.

This leads me to remark that I have almost always been treated honestly by my reviewers, passing over those without scientific knowledge as not worthy of notice. My views have often been grossly misrepresented, bitterly opposed and ridiculed, but this has been generally done, as I believe, in good faith. On the whole I do not doubt that my works have been over and over again greatly overpraised. I rejoice that I have avoided controversies, and this I owe to Lyell, who many years ago, in reference to my geological works, strongly advised me never to get entangled in a controversy, as it rarely did any good and caused a miserable loss of time and temper.

Whenever I have found out that I have blundered, or that my work has been imperfect, and when I have been contemptuously criticised, and even when I have been overpraised, so that I have felt mortified, it has been my greatest comfort to say hundreds of times to myself that "I have worked as hard and as well as I could, and no man can do more than this." I remember when in Good Success Bay, in Tierra del Fuego, thinking (and, I believe, that I wrote home to the effect) that I could not employ my life better than in adding a little to Natural Science. This I have done to the best of my abilities, and critics may say what they like, but they cannot destroy this conviction.

During the two last months of 1859 I was fully occupied in preparing a second edition of the 'Origin,' and by an enormous correspondence. On January 1st, 1860, I began arranging my notes for my work on the 'Variation of Animals and Plants under Domestication;' but it was not published until the beginning of 1868; the delay having been caused partly by frequent illnesses, one of which lasted seven months, and partly by being tempted to publish on other subjects which at the time interested me more.

On May 15th, 1862, my little book on the 'Fertilisation of Orchids,' which cost me ten months' work, was published: most of the facts had been slowly accumulated during several previous years. During the summer of 1839, and, I believe, during the previous summer, I was led to attend to the cross-fertilisation of flowers by the aid of insects, from having come to the conclusion in my speculations on the origin of species, that crossing played an important part in keeping specific forms constant. I attended to the subject more or less during every subsequent summer; and my interest in it was greatly enhanced by having procured and read in November 1841, through the advice of Robert Brown, a copy of C.K. Sprengel's wonderful book, 'Das entdeckte Geheimniss der Natur.' For some years before 1862 I had specially attended to the fertilisation of our British orchids; and it seemed to me the best plan to prepare as complete a treatise on this group of plants as well as I could, rather than to utilise the great mass of matter which I had slowly collected with respect to other plants.

My resolve proved a wise one; for since the

appearance of my book, a surprising number of papers and separate works on the fertilisation of all kinds of flowers have appeared: and these are far better done than I could possibly have effected. The merits of poor old Sprengel, so long overlooked, are now fully recognised many years after his death.

During the same year I published in the 'Journal of the Linnean Society' a paper "On the Two Forms, or Dimorphic Condition of Primula," and during the next five years, five other papers on dimorphic and trimorphic plants. I do not think anything in my scientific life has given me so much satisfaction as making out the meaning of the structure of these plants. I had noticed in 1838 or 1839 the dimorphism of Linum flavum, and had at first thought that it was merely a case of unmeaning variability. But on examining the common species of Primula I found that the two forms were much too regular and constant to be thus viewed. I therefore became almost convinced that the common cowslip and primrose were on the high road to become dioecious;—that the short pistil in the one form, and the short stamens in the other form were tending towards abortion. The plants were therefore subjected under this point of view to trial; but as soon as the flowers with short pistils fertilised with pollen from the short stamens, were found to yield more seeds than any other of the four possible unions, the abortion-theory was knocked on the head. After some additional experiment, it became evident that the two forms, though both were perfect hermaphrodites, bore almost the same relation to one another as do the two sexes of an ordinary animal. With Lythrum we have the still more wonderful case of three forms standing in a similar relation to one another. I afterwards found that the offspring from the union of two plants belonging to the same forms presented a close and curious analogy with hybrids from the union of two distinct species.

In the autumn of 1864 I finished a long paper on 'Climbing Plants,' and sent it to the Linnean Society. The writing of this paper cost me four months; but I was so unwell when I received the proof-sheets that I was forced to leave them very badly and often obscurely expressed. The paper was little noticed, but when in 1875 it was corrected and published as a separate book it sold well. I was led to take up this subject by reading a short paper by Asa Gray, published in 1858. He sent me seeds, and on raising some plants I was so much fascinated and perplexed by the revolving movements of the tendrils and stems, which movements are really very simple, though appearing at first sight very complex, that I procured various other kinds of climbing plants, and studied the whole subject. I was all the more attracted to it, from not being at all satisfied with the explanation which Henslow gave us in his lectures, about twining plants, namely, that they had a natural tendency to grow up in a spire. This explanation proved quite erroneous. Some of the adaptations displayed by Climbing Plants are as beautiful as those of Orchids for ensuring cross-fertilisation.

My 'Variation of Animals and Plants under Domestication' was begun, as already stated, in the beginning of 1860, but was not published until the beginning of 1868. It was a big book, and cost me four years and two months' hard labour. It gives all my observations and an immense number of facts collected from various sources, about our domestic productions. In the second volume the causes and laws of variation, inheritance, etc., are discussed as far as our present state of knowledge permits. Towards the end of the work I give my well-abused hypothesis of Pangenesis. An unverified hypothesis is of little or no value; but if anyone should hereafter be led to make observations by which some such hypothesis could be established, I shall have done good service, as an astonishing number of isolated facts can be thus connected together and rendered intelligible. In 1875 a second and largely corrected edition, which cost me a good deal of labour, was brought out.

My 'Descent of Man' was published in February, 1871. As soon as I had become, in the year 1837 or 1838, convinced that species were mutable productions, I could not avoid the belief that man must come under the same law. Accordingly I collected notes on the subject for my own satisfaction, and not for a long time with any intention of publishing. Although in the 'Origin of Species' the derivation of any particular species is never discussed, yet I thought it best, in order that no honourable man should accuse me of concealing my views, to add that by the work "light would be thrown on the origin of man and his history." It would have been useless and injurious to the success of the book to have paraded, without giving any evidence, my conviction with respect to his origin.

But when I found that many naturalists fully accepted the doctrine of the evolution of species, it seemed to me advisable to work up such notes as I possessed, and to publish a special treatise on the origin of man. I was the more glad to do so, as it gave me an opportunity of fully discussing sexual selection—a subject which had always greatly interested me. This subject, and that of the variation of our domestic productions, together with the causes and laws of variation, inheritance, and the intercrossing of plants, are the sole subjects which I have been able to write about in full, so as to use all the materials which I have collected. The 'Descent of Man' took me three years to write, but then as usual some of this time was lost by ill health, and some was consumed by preparing new editions and other minor works. A second and largely corrected edition of the 'Descent' appeared in 1874.

My book on the 'Expression of the Emotions in Men and Animals' was published in the autumn of 1872. I had intended to give only a chapter on the subject in the 'Descent of Man,' but as soon as I began to put my notes together, I saw that it would require a separate treatise.

My first child was born on December 27th, 1839, and I at once commenced to make notes on the first dawn of the various expressions which he exhibited, for I felt convinced, even at this early period, that the most complex and fine shades of expression must all have had a gradual and natural origin. During the summer of the following year, 1840, I read Sir C. Bell's admirable work on expression, and this greatly increased the interest which I felt in the subject, though I could not at all agree with his belief that various muscles had been specially created for the sake of expression. From this time forward I occasionally attended to the subject, both with respect to man and our domesticated animals. My book sold largely; 5267 copies having been disposed of on the day of publication.

In the summer of 1860 I was idling and resting near Hartfield, where two species of Drosera abound; and I noticed that numerous insects had been entrapped by the leaves. I carried home some plants, and on giving them insects saw the movements of the tentacles, and this made me think it probable that the insects were caught for some special purpose. Fortunately a crucial test occurred to me, that of placing a large number of leaves in various nitrogenous and non-nitrogenous fluids of equal density; and as soon as I found that the former alone excited energetic movements, it was obvious that here was a fine new field for investigation.

During subsequent years, whenever I had leisure, I pursued my experiments, and my book on 'Insectivorous Plants' was published in July 1875—

that is, sixteen years after my first observations. The delay in this case, as with all my other books, has been a great advantage to me; for a man after a long interval can criticise his own work, almost as well as if it were that of another person. The fact that a plant should secrete, when properly excited, a fluid containing an acid and ferment, closely analogous to the digestive fluid of an animal, was certainly a remarkable discovery.

During this autumn of 1876 I shall publish on the 'Effects of Cross and Self-Fertilisation in the Vegetable Kingdom.' This book will form a complement to that on the 'Fertilisation of Orchids,' in which I showed how perfect were the means for cross-fertilisation, and here I shall show how important are the results. I was led to make, during eleven years, the numerous experiments recorded in this volume, by a mere accidental observation; and indeed it required the accident to be repeated before my attention was thoroughly aroused to the remarkable fact that seedlings of self-fertilised parentage are inferior, even in the first generation, in height and vigour to seedlings of cross-fertilised parentage. I hope also to republish a revised edition of my book on Orchids, and hereafter my papers on dimorphic and trimorphic plants, together with some additional observations on allied points which I never have had time to arrange. My strength will then probably be exhausted, and I shall be ready to exclaim "Nunc dimittis."

Written May 1st, 1881.

'The Effects of Cross and Self-Fertilisation' was published in the autumn of 1876; and the results there arrived at explain, as I believe, the endless and wonderful contrivances for the transportal of pollen from one plant to another of the same species. I now believe, however, chiefly from the observations of Hermann Muller, that I ought to have insisted more strongly than I did on the many adaptations for self-fertilisation; though I was well aware of many such adaptations. A much enlarged edition of my 'Fertilisation of Orchids' was published in 1877.

In this same year 'The Different Forms of Flowers, etc.,' appeared, and in 1880 a second edition. This book consists chiefly of the several papers on Heterostyled flowers originally published by the Linnean Society, corrected, with much new matter added, together with observations on some other cases in which the same plant bears two kinds of flowers. As before remarked, no little discovery of mine ever gave me so much pleasure as the making out the meaning of heterostyled flowers. The results of crossing such flowers in an illegitimate manner, I believe to be very important, as bearing on the sterility of hybrids; although these results have been noticed by only a few persons.

In 1879, I had a translation of Dr. Ernst Krause's 'Life of Erasmus Darwin' published, and I added a sketch of his character and habits from material in my possession. Many persons have been much interested by this little life, and I am surprised that only 800 or 900 copies were sold.

In 1880 I published, with [my son] Frank's assistance, our 'Power of Movement in Plants.' This was a tough piece of work. The book bears somewhat the same relation to my little book on 'Climbing Plants,' which 'Cross-Fertilisation' did to the 'Fertilisation of Orchids;' for in accordance with the principle of evolution it was impossible to account for climbing plants having been developed in so many widely different groups unless all kinds of plants possess some slight power of movement of an analogous kind. This I proved to be the case; and I was further led to a rather wide generalisation, viz. that the great and important classes of movements, excited by light, the attraction of gravity, etc., are all modified forms of the fundamental movement of circumnutation. It has always pleased me to exalt plants in the scale of organised beings; and I therefore felt an especial pleasure in showing how many and what admirably well adapted movements the tip of a root possesses.

I have now (May 1, 1881) sent to the printers the MS. of a little book on 'The Formation of Vegetable Mould, through the Action of Worms.' This is a subject of but small importance; and I know not whether it will interest any readers (Between November 1881 and February 1884, 8500 copies have been sold.), but it has interested me. It is the completion of a short paper read before the Geological Society more than forty years ago, and has revived old geological thoughts.

I have now mentioned all the books which I have published, and these have been the milestones in my life, so that little remains to be said. I am not conscious of any change in my mind during the last thirty years, excepting in one point presently to be mentioned; nor, indeed, could any change have been expected unless one of general deterioration. But my father lived to his eighty-third year with his mind as lively as ever it was, and all his faculties undimmed; and I hope that I may die before my mind fails to a sensible extent. I think that I have become a little more skilful in guessing right explanations and in devising experimental tests; but this may probably be the result of mere practice, and of a larger store of knowledge. I have as much difficulty as ever in expressing myself clearly and concisely; and this difficulty has caused me a very great loss of time; but it has had the compensating advantage of forcing me to think long and intently about every sentence, and thus I have been led to see errors in reasoning and in my own observations or those of others.

There seems to be a sort of fatality in my mind leading me to put at first my statement or proposition in a wrong or awkward form. Formerly I used to think about my sentences before writing them down; but for several years I have found that it saves time to scribble in a vile hand whole pages as quickly as I possibly can, contracting half the words; and then correct deliberately. Sentences thus scribbled down are often better ones than I could have written deliberately.

Having said thus much about my manner of writing, I will add that with my large books I spend a good deal of time over the general arrangement of the matter. I first make the rudest outline in two or three pages, and then a larger one in several pages, a few words or one word standing for a whole discussion or series of facts. Each one of these headings is again enlarged and often transferred before I begin to write in extenso. As in several of my books facts observed by others have been very extensively used, and as I have always had several quite distinct subjects in hand at the same time, I may mention that I keep from thirty to forty large portfolios, in cabinets with labelled shelves, into which I can at once put a detached reference or memorandum. I have bought many books, and at their ends I make an index of all the facts that concern my work; or, if the book is not my own, write out a separate abstract, and of such abstracts I have a large drawer full. Before beginning on any subject I look to all the short indexes and make a general and classified index, and by taking the one or more proper portfolios I have all the information collected during my life ready for use.

I have said that in one respect my mind has changed during the last twenty or thirty years. Up to the age of thirty, or beyond it, poetry of many kinds, such as the works of Milton, Gray, Byron, Wordsworth, Coleridge, and Shelley, gave me great pleasure, and even as a schoolboy I took intense delight in Shakespeare, especially in the historical plays. I have also said that formerly pictures gave me considerable, and music very great delight. But now for many years I cannot endure to read a line of poetry: I have tried lately to read Shakespeare, and found it so intolerably dull that it nauseated me. I have also almost lost my taste for pictures or music. Music generally sets me thinking too energetically on what I have been at work on, instead of giving me pleasure. I retain some taste for fine scenery, but it does not cause me the exquisite delight which it formerly did. On the other hand, novels which are works of the imagination, though not of a very high order, have been for years a wonderful relief and pleasure to me, and I often bless all novelists. A surprising number have been read aloud to me, and I like all if moderately good, and if they do not end unhappily—against which a law ought to be passed. A novel, according to my taste, does not come into the first class unless it contains some person whom one can thoroughly love, and if a pretty woman all the better.

This curious and lamentable loss of the higher aesthetic tastes is all the odder, as books on history, biographies, and travels (independently of any scientific facts which they may contain), and essays on all sorts of subjects interest me as much as ever they did. My mind seems to have become a kind of machine for grinding general laws out of large collections of facts, but why this should have caused the atrophy of that part of the brain alone, on which the higher tastes depend, I cannot conceive. A man with a mind more highly organised or better constituted than mine, would not, I suppose, have thus suffered; and if I had to live my life again, I would have made a rule to read some poetry and listen to some music at least once every week; for perhaps the parts of my brain now atrophied would thus have been kept active through use. The loss of these tastes is a loss of happiness, and may possibly be injurious to the intellect, and more probably to the moral character, by enfeebling the emotional part of our nature.

My books have sold largely in England, have been translated into many languages, and passed through several editions in foreign countries. I have heard it said that the success of a work abroad is the best test of its enduring value. I doubt whether this is at all trustworthy; but judged by this standard my name ought to last for a few years. Therefore it may be worth while to try to analyse the mental qualities and the conditions on which my success has depended; though I am aware that no man can do this correctly.

I have no great quickness of apprehension or

wit which is so remarkable in some clever men, for instance, Huxley. I am therefore a poor critic: a paper or book, when first read, generally excites my admiration, and it is only after considerable reflection that I perceive the weak points. My power to follow a long and purely abstract train of thought is very limited; and therefore I could never have succeeded with metaphysics or mathematics. My memory is extensive, yet hazy: it suffices to make me cautious by vaguely telling me that I have observed or read something opposed to the conclusion which I am drawing, or on the other hand in favour of it; and after a time I can generally recollect where to search for my authority. So poor in one sense is my memory, that I have never been able to remember for more than a few days a single date or a line of poetry.

Some of my critics have said, "Oh, he is a good observer, but he has no power of reasoning!" I do not think that this can be true, for the 'Origin of Species' is one long argument from the beginning to the end, and it has convinced not a few able men. No one could have written it without having some power of reasoning. I have a fair share of invention, and of common sense or judgment, such as every fairly successful lawyer or doctor must have, but not, I believe, in any higher degree.

On the favourable side of the balance, I think that I am superior to the common run of men in noticing things which easily escape attention, and in observing them carefully. My industry has been nearly as great as it could have been in the observation and collection of facts. What is far more important, my love of natural science has been steady and ardent.

This pure love has, however, been much aided by the ambition to be esteemed by my fellow naturalists. From my early youth I have had the strongest desire to understand or explain whatever I observed,—that is, to group all facts under some general laws. These causes combined have given me the patience to reflect or ponder for any number of years over any unexplained problem. As far as I can judge, I am not apt to follow blindly the lead of other men. I have steadily endeavoured to keep my mind free so as to give up any hypothesis, however much beloved (and I cannot resist forming one on every subject), as soon as facts are shown to be opposed to it. Indeed, I have had no choice but to act in this manner, for with the exception of the Coral Reefs, I cannot remember a single first-formed hypothesis which had not after a time to be given up or greatly modified. This has naturally led me to distrust greatly deductive reasoning in the mixed sciences. On the other hand, I am not very sceptical,—a frame of mind which I believe to be injurious to the progress of science. A good deal of scepticism in a scientific man is advisable to avoid much loss of time, but I have met with not a few men, who, I feel sure, have often thus been deterred from experiment or observations, which would have proved directly or indirectly serviceable.

In illustration, I will give the oddest case which I have known. A gentleman (who, as I afterwards heard, is a good local botanist) wrote to me from the Eastern counties that the seed or beans of the common field-bean had this year everywhere grown on the wrong side of the pod. I wrote back, asking for further information, as I did not understand what was meant; but I did not receive any answer for a very long time. I then saw in two newspapers, one published in Kent and the other in Yorkshire, paragraphs stating that it was a most remarkable fact that "the beans this year had all grown on the wrong side." So I thought there must be some foundation for so general a statement. Accordingly, I went to my gardener, an old Kentish man, and asked him whether he had heard anything about it, and he answered, "Oh, no, sir, it must be a mistake, for the beans grow on the wrong side only on leap-year, and this is not leap-year." I then asked him how they grew in common years and how on leap-years, but soon found that he knew absolutely nothing of how they grew at any time, but he stuck to his belief.

After a time I heard from my first informant, who, with many apologies, said that he should not have written to me had he not heard the statement from several intelligent farmers; but that he had since spoken again to every one of them, and not one knew in the least what he had himself meant. So that here a belief—if indeed a statement with no definite idea attached to it can be called a belief—had spread over almost the whole of England without any vestige of evidence.

I have known in the course of my life only three intentionally falsified statements, and one of these may have been a hoax (and there have been several scientific hoaxes) which, however, took in an American Agricultural Journal. It related to the formation in Holland of a new breed of oxen by the crossing of distinct species of Bos (some of which I happen to know are sterile together), and the author had the impudence to state that he had corresponded with me, and that I had been deeply impressed with the importance of his result. The article was sent to me by the editor of an English Agricultural Journal, asking for my opinion before republishing it.

A second case was an account of several varieties, raised by the author from several species of Primula, which had spontaneously yielded a full complement of seed, although the parent plants had been carefully protected from the access of insects. This account was published before I had discovered the meaning of heterostylism, and the whole statement must have been fraudulent, or there was neglect in excluding insects so gross as to be scarcely credible.

The third case was more curious: Mr. Huth published in his book on 'Consanguineous Marriage' some long extracts from a Belgian author, who stated that he had interbred rabbits in the closest manner for very many generations, without the least injurious effects. The account was published in a most respectable Journal, that of the Royal Society of Belgium; but I could not avoid feeling doubts—I hardly know why, except that there were no accidents of any kind, and my experience in breeding animals made me think this very improbable.

So with much hesitation I wrote to Professor Van Beneden, asking him whether the author was a trustworthy man. I soon heard in answer that the Society had been greatly shocked by discovering that the whole account was a fraud. (The falseness of the published statements on which Mr. Huth relied has been pointed out by himself in a slip inserted in all the copies of his book which then remained unsold.) The writer had been publicly challenged in the Journal to say where he had resided and kept his large stock of rabbits while carrying on his experiments, which must have consumed several years, and no answer could be extracted from him.

My habits are methodical, and this has been of not a little use for my particular line of work. Lastly, I have had ample leisure from not having to earn my own bread. Even ill-health, though it has annihilated several years of my life, has saved me from the distractions of society and amusement.

Therefore my success as a man of science, whatever this may have amounted to, has been determined, as far as I can judge, by complex and diversified mental qualities and conditions. Of these, the most important have been—the love of science—unbounded patience in long reflecting over any subject—industry in observing and collecting facts—and a fair share of invention as well as of common sense. With such moderate abilities as I possess, it is truly surprising that I should have influenced to a considerable extent the belief of scientific men on some important points.